001
SWORD
ART
ONLINE
PROGRESSIVE
ART: KISEKI HIMURA
ORIGINAL STORY: REKI KAWAHARA
CHARACTER DESIGN: abec

SWORD ART ONLINE PROGRESSIVE 001

CONTENTS

IF I KEEP FIGHTING LIKE THIS...

...THE DAY WILL COME WHEN I FINALLY COL-LAPSE.

チャキン

CHAKIN (SHKING)

BUT UNTIL THAT MOMENT ...
#001: Like a Shooting Star

...I'M GOING TO KEEP RUNNING.
SO I CAN PROVE...
...THAT I GAVE EVERY-THING I HAD.

THEN I'LL DISAP-PEAR.
BURN AWAY IN THE ATMO-SPHERE.
LIKE A FLEETING SHOOTING STAR—!!

チュン
CHUN (CHIRP)
チュン
CHUN

ピッ
PI (BEEP)
2022 11 16
YEAR MONTH DAY
ピッ
PI

MIS-TRESS.

GOOD MORNING. YOUR BREAKFAST IS PREPARED AND READY FOR YOU.

GOOD MORNING, SADA-SAN.
THANK YOU FOR LETTING ME KNOW.

GOOD MORNING, MOM.
GATA (THUNK)
YOU'RE LATE, ASUNA.
I'VE ALREADY EATEN.

PERA (FLIP)
YOU MUST HAVE BEEN UP LATE STUDYING LAST NIGHT.
HOW IS THAT GOING?

IT'S GOOD.
I WAS FIRST IN THE SCHOOL DISTRICT ON THE LAST MOCK TEST.
AND THEY'RE GOING TO ANNOUNCE THE RESULTS OF THE MIDTERMS TODAY.

AS LONG AS I'M IN THE TOP TEN, I CAN GET INTO ANY SCHOOL, AND IF I KEEP STRAIGHT "A"S UNTIL THE FINAL EXAMS...

LISTEN, DEAR.
KACHA (CLINK)

WHY FOCUS ON YOUR HIGH SCHOOL ENTRANCE EXAMS?
IT'S THE COLLEGE ONES THAT COUNT. YOU NEED TO MOVE ON AND GET STARTED ON THE HIGH SCHOOL CURRICULUM.
OKAY ...

PERHAPS WE SHOULD HAVE SENT YOU TO KOUICHIROU'S UNIFIED SCHOOL INSTEAD.
I'M MAKING GOOD PROGRESS IN ENGLISH AND MATH.
カチャ
KACHA (CLINK)
TIME TO EAT.

UNIFIED SCHOOL: A SCHOOL THAT COMBINES MIDDLE AND HIGH SCHOOL TO PROVIDE MORE STREAMLINED PREPARATION FOR COLLEGE ENTRANCE EXAMS.

ガタン
GATAN (KATHUNK)
ゴトン
GOTON (KATHONK)

YUUKI-SENPAI!

GOOD MORNING!
MORN-ING.
I HEARD YOU WERE FIRST ON THE MOCK TEST AGAIN, SENPAI!
CONGRATU-LATIONS!
THANK YOU.
ガタン
GATAN
ゴトン
GOTON
ガタン
GATAN (KATHUNK)
ゴトン
GOTON (KATHONK)

OH! LOOK, SENPAI!
HAVE YOU HEARD OF THIS?
?
SWORD ART ONLINE!

THEY SIMULATE ALL FIVE SENSES AND INPUT THEM DIRECTLY INTO YOUR BRAIN!
IT'S SUP-POSED TO BE SUPER REALIS-TIC!
SWORD ART ONLI
ソードアート・オンライン
10.31 On Sale
I WISH I COULD TRY IT...
I THINK MY BROTHER MENTIONED THAT GAME TO ME TOO.

YOU WANT TO TRY PLAYING IT TOGETHER, SENPAI?
NO.
I'VE GOT EXAMS TO STUDY FOR.

THAT'S NO FUN. I THOUGHT YOU WERE BREEZING THROUGH YOUR TESTS.

BESIDES, PLAYING GAMES IS JUST A WASTE OF YOUR TIME.

YOU KNOW HIGH SCHOOL EXAMS AREN'T THE END GOAL OF LIFE, RIGHT?

YOU DON'T WANT THE PEOPLE FROM THE UNIFIED SCHOOLS TO PULL AHEAD BECAUSE YOU'RE BUSY PLAYING WITH *KIDS' TOYS*, DO YOU?

2022 Senior Class
Second Semester
Midterm
Winter Courses
Committee

I'M NOT THERE.

WHY NOT?
NO WAY...

HEY, DID YOU HEAR...
...THE RUMORS ABOUT YUUKI-SAN?
I TO-TALLY DID!
SUPPOSEDLY SHE GOT SUCKED INTO SOME NEW VIDEO GAME AND STOPPED STUDYING.
WELL, NO WONDER SHE FELL FROM THE TOP RANKS...
HEE HEE!
BUT WHY A STUPID VIDEO GAME?
HEE HEE!
ISN'T THAT FOR KIDS?
WHAT DOES THIS MEAN? IS SHE SECRETLY ONE OF THOSE OTAKU?
THAT IS SO CREEPY!
HA-HA!
GOOD FOR US, THOUGH, RIGHT? THAT'S ONE EXTRA SPOT FOR US TO SLIP INTO!
AHA-HA!
HEE HEE!

OH, BUT JUST LISTEN TO THIS! THE TRUTH IS...
ARE YOU FOR REAL?
YES, IT'S TRUE...
HILARI-OUS!
SHE WAS ACTING ALL COOL, LIKE "PLAYING GAMES IS A WASTE OF YOUR TIME"...
OH, SHE'S LOOKING THIS WAY!
...THEN SHE GOES AND STARTS PLAYING ONE, ONLY TO GET TRAPPED INSIDE...
BFFT!

N-NO, MOM...
SUU (SHH)
HUH ...?
THIS IS ALL A BIG MISTAKE...

A GAME?
A VIDEO GAME?
YOU LITTLE FOOL.
HAVE YOU NO PRIDE AS A YUUKI? HAVE YOU NO SHAME?
NO...
フル
FURU (SHAKE)
フル
FURU
IT'S NOT LIKE THAT...
I DIDN'T MEAN TO...

I WANT TO GO HOME!
You will only be released under one condition—
I JUST WANT TO GO HOME!
Defeat the game.

NOVEMBER 19TH, 2022.
チッ
CHI (TICK)
SATUR-DAY.
チッ
CHI
チッ
CHI

TODAY IS THE DAY...
...OF THE UNIFIED MOCK TEST...

HAVE A GOOD DAY.
TAKE CARE.

ペコリ
PEKORI (BOW)

カラン
KARAN (CLANK)
コロン
KORON (CLUNK)
ぐい
GUI (TUG)
カチャ
KACHA (CLINK)
カチャ
KACHA
ガヤ
GAYA (MURMUR)
ガヤ
GAYA

ガヤ
GAYA
ワイ
WAI (CHATTER)
ワイ
WAI
ガヤ
GAYA

Purchase
Black Bread x1
1 C
ピコン
PIKON (BEEP)
COME AGAIN!

ペコリ
PEKORI (BOW)

ザワ
GAYA
GAYA
ザワ
WHY DO I GET HUNGRY...
...IN A STUPID GAME?
IT'S RIDICULOUS.
ザワ
GAYA
GAYA

MUGU (MUNCH)
むぐ むぐ
MUGU
IT DOESN'T EVEN TASTE GOOD.

I WANT TO EAT SADA-SAN'S COOKING AGAIN.
A HIDDEN LOG-OUT SPOT?

GAYA (CHATTER)
GAYA
IT'S JUST ANOTHER FALSE RUMOR, OBVIOUSLY.
BUT I HEAR IT COMES FROM THE "RAT" HERSELF.
OH YEAH?
ZAWA (MURMUR)
ZAWA

SO...
...IT'S SUPPOSED TO BE IN THE FOREST TO THE WEST?
YEAH, THERE'S A CAVE WAY IN THE BACK THAT LOOKS LIKE THE RIGHT PLACE...

AND NO ONE WHO'S GONE HAS COME BACK. SO WHAT DOES THAT SAY?
SOUNDS LIKE THEY GOT KILLED BY MON-STERS, IF YOU ASK ME...

KUWA (SHOVE)
UM!
EX-CUSE ME!
BIKU (FLINCH)
BIKU
WHERE'S THE FOREST TO THE WEST!?
GATA (THUMP)

HUH? UM...
JUST WHERE YOU'D THINK.

ONLY TAKES ABOUT AN HOUR DOWN THE PATH OUT OF THE WEST GATE.
THANK YOU VERY MUCH.
UM, YOU KNOW YOU NEED TO BE ABOUT LEVEL THREE AROUND THERE, RIGHT?

YOU'RE ONE OF THOSE FOLKS WAITING FOR HELP FROM OUTSIDE, RIGHT?
DON'T GET YOURSELF HURT.

NO NEED TO RUSH. IN ANOTHER FEW DAYS, WE'LL ALL BE RESCUED...

THAT'S NO GOOD!
IT WON'T BE IN TIME.

WHAT, YOU GOT URGENT BUSINESS BACK IN REAL LIFE?

URU (SNIFF)

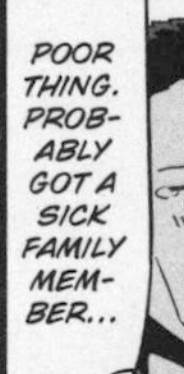
POOR THING. PROBABLY GOT A SICK FAMILY MEMBER...

YES.

TODAY IS...

...THE DAY OF MY...
...HIGH SCHOOL MOCK EXAM!

DAAAH!
HA-HA-HA-HA-HA-HA-HA!!
A MOCK TEST!? NOT EVEN A REAL ONE!
URK.
PFFT!
YEAH, SOUNDS LIKE A REAL PROBLEM TO ME!!
AHA-HA-HA!

ブルルッ
BRRH!
ガリッ
GARI
(SCRAPE)

...
NOSHI
NOSHI
(PLOD)

SA
(SWISH)
SA
SA
SA
JIII
(STARE)

FOUND IT!

HERE'S THE SPOT.

コオオオオ
KOOO (WHOOOSH)
GULP

IT'S JUST A GAME!

I NEED TO GET ...
カチャ
KACHA (CLINK)
... OUT OF HERE.
KIII (CREAK)

SQUISH?

WHAT IS THIS...?

HA (HUFF)

HA

ダラー…

DARAA (DRIP)

OH ...
OH NO.

PARA
(SPRINKLE)

PARA

WHAT IS THIS? I CAN'T MOVE...

GATA
(RATTLE)

GATA

PI
(BEEP)

AM I GOING TO DIE?

PI

I DIDN'T LIVE...
SIGN: MIDDLE SCHOOL CRAM CENTER
...THROUGH FIFTEEN YEARS OF HARD WORK...
...FOR THIS HOR-RIBLE ENDING.
THIS SUCKS.
NO WAY—

ZUDAMU
(CZWAMM)

ZURU
(SHLUNK)

PAAN
(CRAASH)

...WHO ...?
IT'S OVER.
ヒュン ヒュン
HYUN (SWISH)
HYUN
CHAKIN (SHE-KING)
HEY, NICE WORK!
TEKU (TEK)
TEKU
GOTTA SAY, I REALLY DON'T APPRECIATE FOLKS SPREADING FALSE RUMORS USING MY NAME.
IT'S A HARD BUSINESS BEING AN INFORMANT.
IS OUR NEWBIE HERE STILL ALIVE?
ZUI (PEER)
OH GOOD, SHE IS.
DOSA (THUMP)
HERE, DRINK THIS HEALING POT.
ON THE HOUSE.
KYUPO (SHUP)
ALL RIGHT, I'M OFF.
YOU CAN DEAL WITH YOUR IM-POSTOR ON YOUR OWN. I DON'T WANNA GO ORANGE.
POT: SHORT FOR "POTION." AN ABBREVIATION FOR FASTER TYPING IN ONLINE GAMES.
NMMG!
GULP, GULP!
YEAH, I KNOW.
HIRA
HIRA (WAVE)
DON'T FORGET ABOUT THE OTHER THING. SO LONG.
ZA (ZSH)

JUS WHAT SOUNI LIKE.

IT'S A JOB BUYING AND SELLING INTELLIGENCE.

I GATHER ALL KINDS OF INFO...

...THEN PROVIDE IT AT A REASONABLE PRICE.

IF IT BENEFITS THE PUBLIC, I SPREAD IT...

...OR IF NEEDED, BURY IT FOREVER.

BY THE WAY, WHAT I JUST TOLD YOU...

...COSTS TEN COL.

...HA HA.
THAT'S WEIRD.
THIS IS A GAME ...
... BUT IT FEELS LIKE REALITY.

WELL, OF COURSE.
THIS IS OUR REALITY NOW.

MISS INFOR-MANT...
IS THE "HIDDEN LOG OUT"...
...JUST A FALSE RUMOR?

SORRY.
GYU (SQUEEZE)
THERE'S NO SUCH THING.

IN THAT CASE ...
... PLEASE SELL ME SOME INFO.

I WANT TO KNOW HOW TO BE STRON-GER.

PASA (FLAP)
IS THAT ...
...IN ORDER TO SURVIVE LONGER?

NO.

SO THAT...

...I DON'T EVER REGRET ANYTHING AGAIN.

UMM.
PARA (FLIP)
TOKO TOKO (TIPTOE)
"FRENZIED BOAR"...
SNORT?
...A.K.A. "BLUE BOAR," IS A NON-ACTIVE ...?
TEKU TEKU (TEK)
I SEE. IF I DON'T ATTACK THE MONSTER, IT WON'T BE HOSTILE TO ME.
PARA PARA
NON-ACTIVE MEANS ...
TEKU TEKU
KURU (SPIN)

BIKU (FLINCH)
THAT SHOULD BE A BIG HELP TO YOU—
ZUDAN (THWAM)

THE SOURCE OF DATA AND PREREQUISITES ARE SOMEWHAT VAGUE. DID THE AUTHOR TEST THIS INFORMATION TO DETERMINE ITS ACCURACY?
S... SORRY.
BUT IT'S AN EXCELLENT GUIDE FOR A STARTING PLAYER. WELL INDEXED, PLENTY OF NOTES, EVEN A FEW IMAGES AND DIAGRAMS.

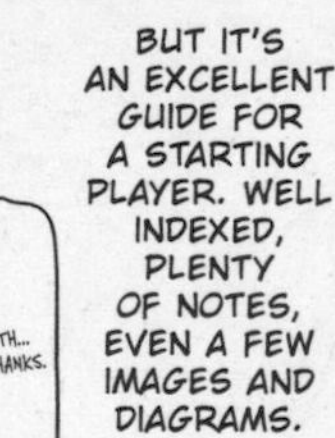
TH... THANKS.

METHODS OF ATTACK— THIS IS A VERY THIN SWORD, SO I WANT... THIS ENTRY.
CHAKI (CHK)
TOKO
SNORT
IT BASICALLY RESEMBLES REGULAR FENCING ...

STARTER SKILL IS "LINEAR."
SURUU (SHING)
FOCUS ON THE TIP AND TWIST...

BYU
(WHOOSH)
ピギィ
PIGII
(SQUEE)
OH.
IT WORKED.
!?
PARIIN
(CRAASH)

THAT WAS FAST!
AND MORE THAN THAT...
I CAN DO IT AFTER ALL.
WELL, I'LL BE.

I TAKE IT BACK.
NO LONGER FREE.
I CAN
GO
GO
GO
GO
SELL THIS
GO (RUMBLE)
AS MY FEE, I DEMAND YOU TELL ME YOUR NAME.

MY NAME?
IT'S ASUNA YUUKI.
W-WAIT, WAIT! SORRY, NEWBIE! I MEANT YOUR PLAYER NAME!!!

I SEE, SO ASUNA IS YOUR PLAYER NAME TOO. WHEN ANYONE MENTIONS NAME, IT'S YOUR PLAYER NAME. I'LL FORGET THAT PIECE OF INFO. JUST BE CAREFUL FROM NOW ON.
KOKU KOKU (NOD)
PAY ATTENTION!
QUEE!
SHUBA (WHOOSH)

ASUNA THE FENCER ...

SHE'LL GO FAR.

THE DAY WILL COME WHEN SHE CATCHES UP TO THE TOP PLAYERS IN THE GAME...
...AND GETS HERSELF A FANTASTIC NICKNAME.

THEN I CAN SELL TODAY'S EVENTS FOR A NICE, HEFTY PRICE.
HEE HEE.
TO SOMEONE OTHER THAN KII-BOY.
HEY...
MISS INFOR-MANT.
HM?

DO YOU SUPPOSE ...

... I COULD DEFEAT THAT MONSTER FROM BEFORE?

FRIDAY, DECEMBER 2ND, 2022

KIIN (CLANG)

KIIN

KIIN

KIIN

KIIN

ZUGAN
(THWAM)

HOW MANY DAYS HAVE PASSED...
...SINCE I WALKED INTO THIS LABY-RINTH?
HUFF
HUFF
BIIIN
(BWINGG)
ビィィィン…

I MIGHT BE FREE OF PHYSICAL EXHAUS-TION...
...BUT I STILL GET MENTALLY FATIGUED.
YORO
YORO
(WOBBLE)
AT TIMES, MY WITS SEEM TO GROW FAINT.

AND WHAT HAPPENS WHEN YOUR CONCEN-TRATION FALTERS...
ZUZUUN
(ZDUMM)
GAKU
(SLUMP)
ガクッ
...IN THE MOST DANGEROUS PART OF A LABYRINTH STUFFED WITH MONSTERS?

THIS HAPPENS, OF COURSE.

GURURURU (GRRR)

GURURU

DAMN.

I DON'T THINK I CAN ESCAPE ...

...THIS PAR-TICULAR AMBUSH.

OH.
A STUN EFFECT.
I GUESS THIS IS IT.

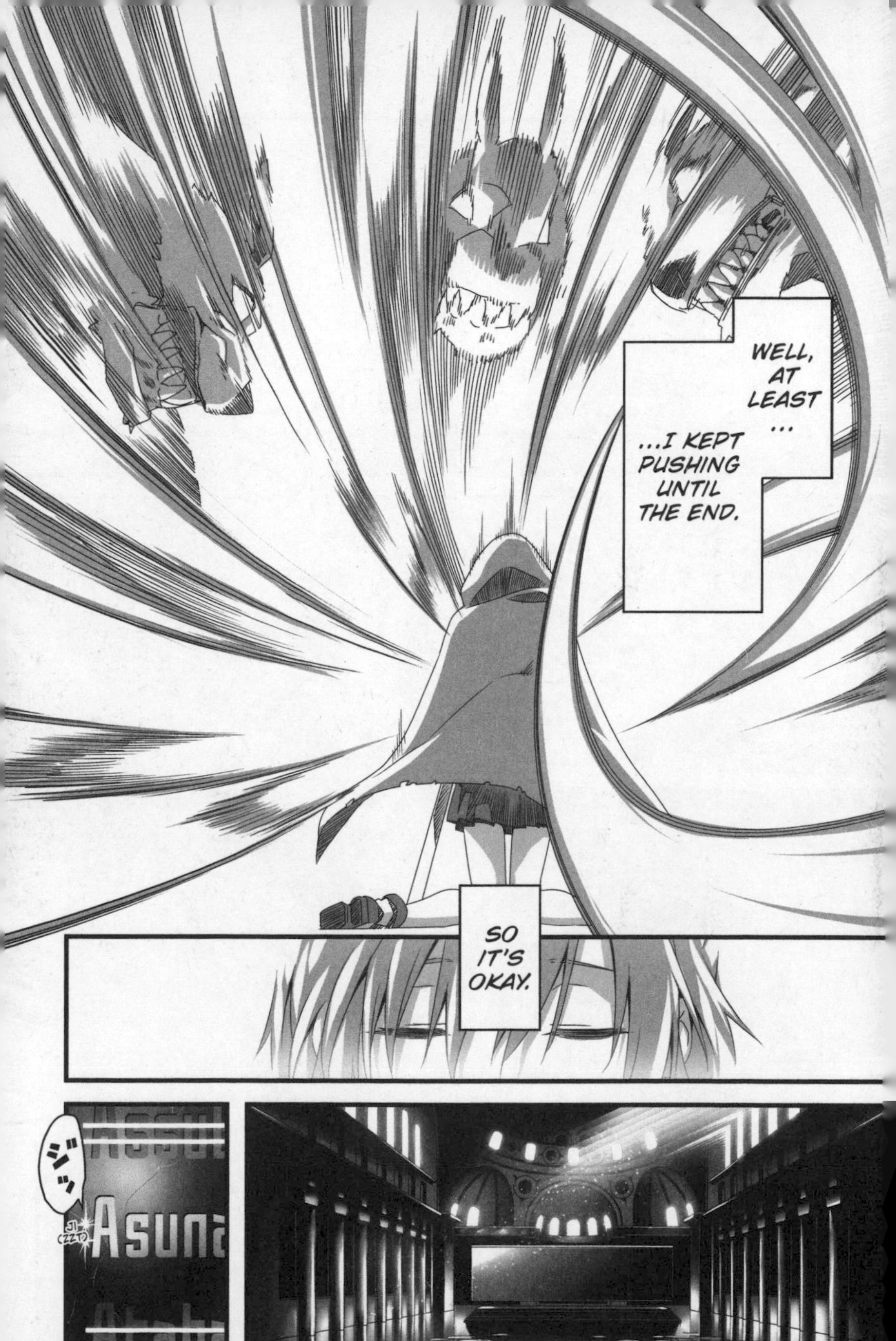
WELL, AT LEAST ...
...I KEPT PUSHING UNTIL THE END.
SO IT'S OKAY.
ジジッ
JI (ZZZT)
Asuna

ZA
(WHOOSH)

WHO ...?
YOU KNOW ...
I DON'T KNOW THIS GUY.
...IF YOU KEEP FIGHTING LIKE THIS, YOU'RE GONNA DIE.
MIND YOUR OWN ...
... BEES-WAX!!

I'M NOT SAYING...

...THAT YOU HAVE TO TREASURE YOUR LIFE OR WHATEVER.

BUT AT LEAST LEAVE ME YOUR MAP DATA. IT WOULD BE A WASTE TO LET THAT DISAPPEAR.

YOU CAN DIE AFTER THAT.

GOT THAT? ON YOUR FEET!
GUGU (HRRG)
UGH ...
HUFF!
HUFF!
YORO (WOBBLE)
GOOD.
THAT'S THE SPIRIT, MISS FENCER.
GURURU (GRRR)
GURURU
GURURU
GURURU
YOU WATCH MY BACK.
WE ATTACK TO-GETH-ER!
DON'T ORDER ME AROUND!
GURURURU
GURURURU
SHEESH!
THREE!
WHO DOES HE THINK HE IS!?
TWO!
ONE!
GO!

#002

JUST ONCE, I ACTUALLY SAW A SHOOTING STAR.

...HERE IN THE MURKY DEPTHS...
#002: Faster Than Anyone

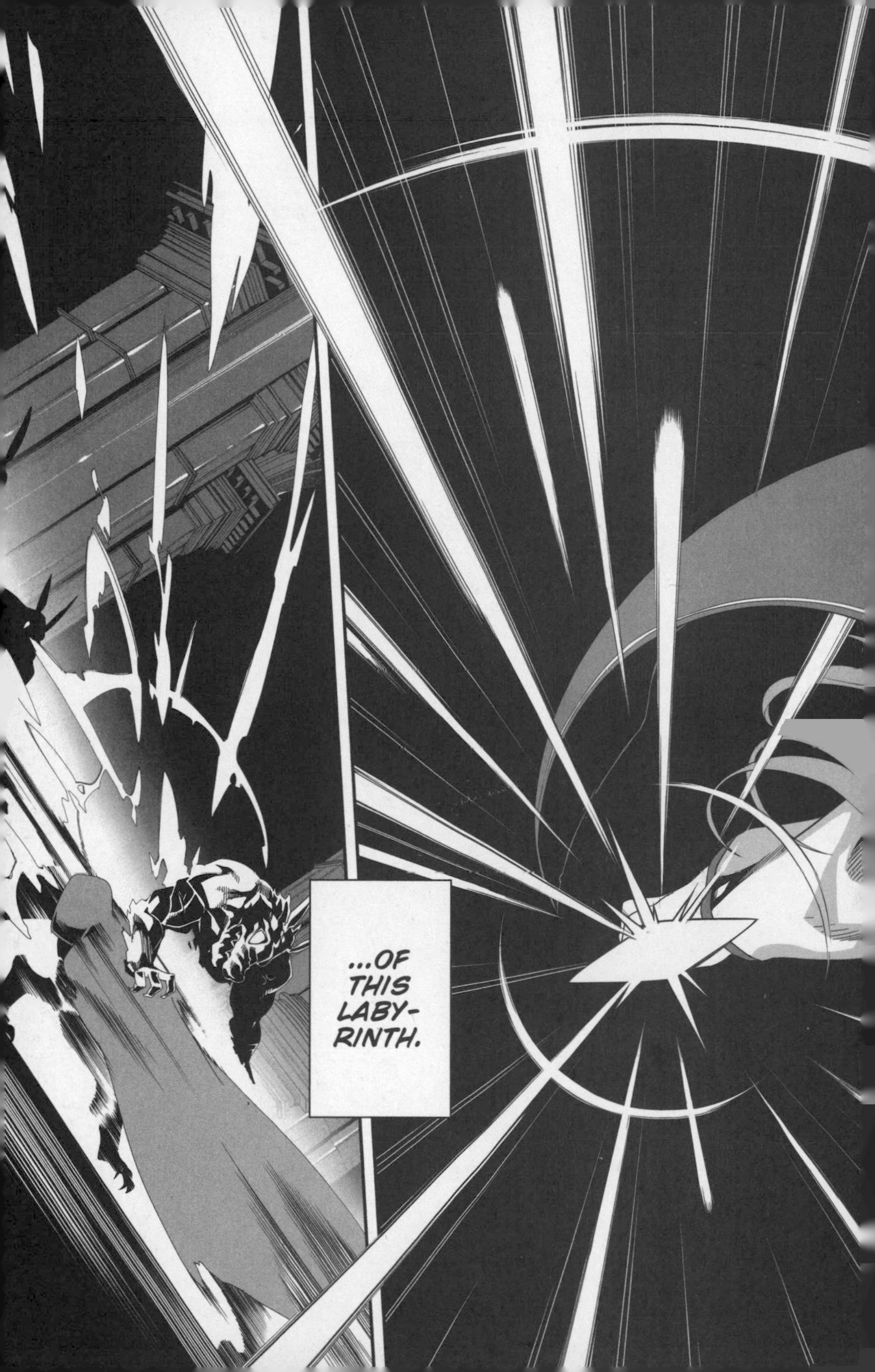
...OF
THIS
LABY-
RINTH.

KYUIII
(WHIRR)
HYUGAGO
(SHWAKAA)

SHE'S FAST!

ZUZAZA (ZWOOSH)

HER SWORD SKILL IS SO PRECISE.

OKAY! THERE'S A WAY OUT NOW!
ぐぐっ
GUGU (HRRG)
ギリ
GIRI (GRIT)
ギリ
GIRI
HURRY AND RUN FOR SAFETY...
ユラリ
YURARI (SWISH)
UM, HELLO?
MISS FENCER?

WHA...
YOU KILLED THEM ALL?
DOSA (THUMP)
!?
KARAN (CLANK)
MISS FENC-ER!!

ガサッ
GASA (RUSTLE)
GOOD MORNING...
... MISS
WHY?

WHY DIDN'T YOU LEAVE ME BEHIND?

YOU'RE FREE TO PURSUE YOUR GLAMOROUS DEATH ALL YOU WANT...
カチャ
KACHA (CLANK)
...BUT AS I TOLD YOU...
...I WANT THAT MAP DATA FIRST.

THEN AGAIN...
...THERE ARE WAYS TO GET AROUND THAT STUFF WHEN THE OTHER PERSON IS ASLEEP.
ピコ
PIKO (BEEP)
ピコ
PIKO
ヌ

ZUPAN (SHWAPP)
EEEP !!?
N... NOTHING! NOTHING AT ALL!!
GO (RUMBLE)
GO
GO
GO
GO
WHAT DID YOU DO TO MY BODY...?
CROSS MY HEART, HOPE TO DIE, DON'T STICK THAT NEEDLE IN MY EYE!!!

YOU...
WANA (TREMBLE) ワナワナ WANA
Y-Y-Y-YOU LIAR!!
YOU USED MY MAP DATA AS AN EXCUSE ...
...TO DO THINGS TO MY BODY, LIKE...
...LIKE THINGS!! THINGS!!
WANA ワナワナ WANA
PURU (TREMBLE) プルプル PURU
N-NO WAY! IT'S A BUM RAP!!!
DRAW YOUR
DAMN
BLADE!!

URK!
GURRRRUGGG

RRRRR

プル
PURU (SHIVER)
プル
PURU
HA-HA-HA-HA-HA! FIRST, WE'D BETTER GET YOU SOME FOOD.
STUPID GAME! STUPID GAME!! STUPID GAME!!!

I-I DON'T NEED IT! I'M NOT GOING TO DIE FROM LACK OF FOOD HERE!

NO WORRIES. THINK OF IT AS AN EXCHANGE FOR YOUR MAP DATA.
カラ
KARA (CLICK)
カラ
KARA

PLUS, YOU CAN'T SAY FOR SURE ...
...THAT YOUR PASSING OUT HAD NOTHING TO DO WITH EXTREME HUNGER.
IF YOU'RE GOING TO TRY YOUR BEST, IT'S WORTH EATING PROPERLY, RIGHT?
PAA (GLOW)

PLUS, THIS IS JUST PLAIN TASTY.
...NOW I'M DOUBTING YOUR SENSE OF TASTE.
IT'S THAT CHEAP BLACK BREAD.

YOU JUST NEED TO THROW IN A LITTLE WRINKLE.
コツン
KOTSUN (TAP)
ポフ
POWA (FWOOP)
WHAT'S THIS?

ヌトー
NUTO (BLORP)

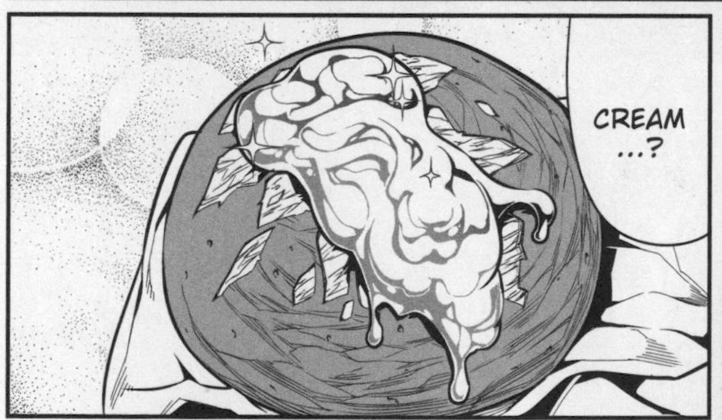
CREAM ...?

GO ON, JUST TRY IT OUT.

はむっ
HAMU (HOMF)
...

BUWA
(WHOOSH)

AAH...

IT'S JUST A
STUPID GAME...

HAGU
(CHOMP)
HAGU

WANT
AN-
OTHER?
BIKU
(FLINCH)

I DIDN'T
SURVIVE
THIS LONG
JUST TO
EAT GOOD
FOOD.
...I'LL
PASS.

WHY, THEN?

SO THAT... I CAN BE MYSELF.

IF I WAS GOING TO JUST HIDE BACK IN THE FIRST CITY...
...AND WASTE AWAY INTO NOTHING...

...THEN I'D RATHER FIGHT WITH ALL OF MY STRENGTH UNTIL THE VERY LAST MOMENT.
AND THEN ...

YOU CAN "DIE SATISFIED"?
I MEAN ...
IT'S A HUNDRED FLOORS!
AFTER TWO MONTHS, WE HAVEN'T EVEN BEATEN THE VERY FIRST ONE!
YOU KNOW HOW MANY PEOPLE HAVE DIED IN THAT TIME?
TWO THOU-SAND!
IT'S IMPOS-SIBLE ...
WE'RE NEVER GOING HOME.

ZAWA (WHOOSH)
ザワ…
ZAWA
I'
S RY.
DID YOU JUST ...?

GONN
(GONG)

GONN
GONN
WHAT'S THAT?
A BELL?
THAT'S THE TOWN...
TOLBANA'S CLOSE BY.

THE BELL STRUCK THREE O'CLOCK. LET'S GO.
?
ZASU
(ZSHH)

GO WHERE?

IT'S TIME FOR THE BOSS BATTLE.

YOU WANNA COME?

PIKU (TWITCH)

WELCOME TO TOLBANA.
...

AT THE AMPHI-THEATER, FOUR O'CLOCK.

KURU (SPIN)
BY THE WAY...

?
...... NEVER MIND.

WAS IT JUST MY IMAGINATION...?
WHAT'S WRONG WITH HIM?
CURI-OUS?

!?

MISS INFORMANT!

YOU CURIOUS ABOUT HIM?

I CAN GIVE YOU THE DETAILS FOR CHEAP, A-CHAN.♡

BA (SWISH)
A- ANYWAY, I ONLY JUST MET HIM!
PLEASE STOP TRYING TO PRY AND START WEIRD RUMORS!
?
AH... I SEE.

OKAY, OKAY, I GET IT.

THANKS FOR THE TIP.

?

ANYWAY, MISS INFORMANT...

...DO YOU KNOW MUCH ABOUT HIM?

OH?

SO YOU WANT TO KNOW MORE ABOUT YOUR WOULD-BE BEAU...
A-CHAN WILL DO ANYTHING ONCE SHE SETS EYES ON HER PRIZE.
UM, WELL...
I HAVE NO IDEA WHERE YOU'RE GETTING THIS IDEA.

OF COURSE, FOR THE RIGHT PRICE, I WOULDN'T BE UNWILLING TO PART WITH THAT INFORMATION.
ピクッ
PIKU (TWITCH)

...
パチクリ
PACHIKURI (BLINK)

コホン
KOHON (AHEM)
HOW-EVER...

...IF YOU BUY HIS INFORMATION FROM ME...
...THAT TRANSACTION BECOMES A NEW PRODUCT FOR ME TO SELL, YOU SEE?
?
YOU KNOW...
JUST BETWEEN YOU AND ME...

WOULD YOU STILL LIKE TO BUY?

NO THANKS!

I HAVE NO INTEREST IN HIM, THANK YOU VERY MUCH!

I SEE.

PON (PAT)

THAT'S GOOD TO HEAR.

?

ZAWA (MURMUR)

TEKU (TEK) TEKU

ZAWA

WOW... LOOK AT ALL THESE PEOPLE...

......!

...KNOWING THEY COULD DIE IN THE ATTEMPT...

KO (TOK)
KO

YOU REALLY THINK...
...THEY'RE ALL DOING IT OUT OF THE GOODNESS OF THEIR HEARTS?
I'M NOT SAYING THERE AREN'T ANY WITH GOOD MOTIVES...

...BUT IF YOU ASK ME...
...MOST OF THEM ARE JUST AFRAID OF BEING LEFT IN THE DUST.

LEFT IN THE DUST? BEHIND WHAT?

BEHIND THE FRONTIER...
ZA (ZSHH)

THE THOUGHT OF DYING IS FRIGHTENING...
...BUT SO IS THE IDEA THAT THE BOSS IS BEING DEFEATED...

...WITHOUT THEM.
I MEAN, I FEEL THE SAME WAY.

IS THAT LIKE ...

...THE SAME KIND OF MOTIVATION THAT...
...YOU NEED TO KEEP YOURSELF IN THE TOP 2% OF THE COUNTRY?
OR TO STAY IN THE TOP TEN OF YOUR YEAR?
UM ...
I... THINK SO?

PAN (CLAP)
PAN
AHH!

THANK YOU ALL FOR HEEDING MY CALL TODAY!
YOU ARE THE BEST AND BRIGHT-EST OF SAO!

I SEE.
IT IS THE SAME THING.

CHASED INTO A CORNER BY SOME-THING YOU CAN'T SEE...
...WITH-OUT A CLEAR GOAL IN SIGHT.

GET INTO A GOOD HIGH SCHOOL, JUST BECAUSE.
GET INTO A GOOD COLLEGE, JUST BECAUSE.
GET A GOOD JOB, JUST BECAUSE.

WHAT HAP-PENS THEN?
...I DON'T KNOW.

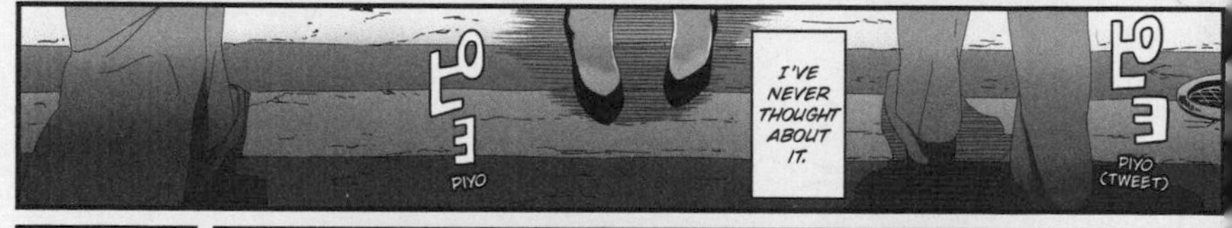
ピヨ
PIYO (TWEET)
I'VE NEVER THOUGHT ABOUT IT.
ピヨ
PIYO

I GUESS...
BUT...
...I'M NO DIFFER-ENT FROM THESE GAME ADDICTS.
HA HA.

MY GOAL RIGHT NOW IS QUITE OBVIOUS.
TO CLEAR THE FIRST FLOOR.
AND UNTIL WE CONQUER ALL ONE HUNDRED OF THEM...
I STRIKE...
GU (TUG)
...QUICKER THAN ANYONE.
AND FLY...
...SWIFTER THAN ANY OTHER.

#003: Front-Runners

THANK YOU ALL FOR HEEDING MY CALL TODAY!

MY NAME'S DIAVEL ...

...AND I LIKE TO THINK OF MYSELF...

...AS PLAYING A "KNIGHT"!

DON (BOOM)

HA-HA-HA!

I BET YOU WANTED TO SAY YOU'RE PLAYING A "HERO"!

TODAY, OUR PARTY DISCOVERED THE FIRST-FLOOR BOSS CHAMBER!

THE TIME HAS COME TO BEAT THE BOSS...

...AND REACH THE SECOND FLOOR!

IT TOOK AN ENTIRE MONTH...

...BUT NOW WE HAVE THE CHANCE TO SHOW EVERYONE THAT SOMEDAY...

...WE CAN BEAT THIS GAME OF DEATH.

ズン
ズン
ZUN (STOMP)
ZUN
GOTTA GET THIS OFFA MY CHEST...
...BEFORE WE CAN START PLAYIN' LIKE WE'RE ALL PALS.

C'MON, YOU COWARDLY BETA TESTERS!

SHOW YER-SELVES!!!

YOU OWE AN APOLOGY TO THE TWO THOUSAND PEOPLE WHO ALREADY DIED...

...BE-CAUSE YOU WERE TOO BUSY HOGGIN' EVERY-THING TO YOUR-SELVES!

NOW GET DOWN ON HANDS AND KNEES TA APOLO-GIZE...

...AND DONATE YOUR STOCK-PILE O' COL AND ITEMS!

MY NAME'S AGIL.
DON (BOOM)
KIBAOU-SAN...
...IF I HAVE THIS RIGHT...
...YOU'RE CLAIMING THAT MANY NEWBIES DIED BECAUSE THE FORMER TESTERS DIDN'T HELP THEM...
...SO THEY OUGHT TO PAY REPARA-TIONS?
IS THAT COR-RECT?
Y... YEAH.
THEY ABANDONED ALL THE NEW PLAYERS WHO DIDN'T KNOW LEFT FROM RIGHT ON THE DAY THIS DAMN GAME STARTED...
...AN' HIGHTAILED IT RIGHT OUTTA THE TOWN OF BEGINNINGS TO PURSUE THEIR OWN SELFISH ENDS.
JIRI (SCRAPE)
YOU KNOW ANYONE AROUND YOU THAT FITS THE BILL?

WHEN THEM BETA ASSHOLES HOGGED ALL THE BEST HUNTIN' GROUNDS AND LUCRATIVE QUESTS...
GIRI (SCRAPE)

...THEY KEPT THE BEGINNERS FROM GOOD LEVELING SPOTS...
...SO THEY HAD TA VENTURE INTA DANGEROUS ZONES AND WOUND UP DEAD.
GI

THAT'S TRUE.
THE RESOURCES AVAILABLE TO PLAYERS IN THIS GAME ARE LIMITED BY THE SYSTEM.

BUT CONSID THIS QUESTI KIBAOU SAN.
IF YOU WERE A SELF-INTERESTED BETA TESTER WHO ONLY CARED ABOUT YOUR OWN SURVIVAL...
...AND YOU COULD MONOPOLIZE ONE THING, WHAT WOULD YOU CHOOSE?
THE BEST HUNTING GROUND? THE LUCRATIVE QUESTS?
WH-WHAT'S YER POINT...?

I'D CHOOSE "INFORMATION."

SAO Strategy
1F. labyrinth
Don't worry. This is Argo's guidebook.

EVERY TIME I REACHED A NEW TOWN, THIS GUIDEBOOK...

...WAS AVAILABLE AT THE ITEM SHOPS.

AND FOR FREE TOO.
I'D SAY EVERYONE HAS MADE USE OF THEM. RIGHT?

IT WAS...
...VERY HELPFUL.
WHA ...?

F-FOR FREE...?

THAT RAT! SHE CHARGED ME FIVE HUNDRED COL A POP!

... HUH?

BUT...

...IT FELT TO ME LIKE IT WAS ALL TOO QUICK.

LISTEN, THE IN-FORMATION WAS OUT THERE.
THERE'S NO BETTER GIFT YOU COULD GIVE A GROUP OF BEGINNERS.

YES, MANY PEOPLE DIED.
BUT THAT WAS BECAUSE THEY ASSUMED SAO WORKED THE SAME WAY AS OTHER MMOS...
...AND FAILED TO PULL BACK WHEN THEY NEEDED TO.

MEANWHILE, WE'VE GOT THE INFORMA-TION FROM THE GUIDE...
...AND WE'RE STILL ALIVE.

HE'S MET HIS MATCH.
YOU ALWAYS FIND THESE PEOPLE...
THE ONES WHO AREN'T HAPPY AND WANT TO DRAG EVERYONE ELSE DOWN WITH THEM.

HE DOESN'T REALIZE THERE'S A ROLE ONLY THE FRONT-RUNNERS CAN PLAY...

YOUR POINT IS WELL-TAKEN...

...KIBAOU-SAN.

BUT ISN'T THIS THE TIME TO LOOK FORWARD?

IF THE FORMER TESTERS ARE GOING TO LEND US THEIR HELP TO DEFEAT THE BOSS...

GU (CLENCH)

...WHAT GREATER ALLY COULD WE POSSIBLY HOPE FOR?

DIAVEL-SAN!

NOW, DO YOU MIND?

IF WE CAN GET BACK TO THE TOPIC...

D...
DIAVEL-SAN!
SAO Strategy Gu
1F. BOSS
LOOK ...!
GASA (RUSTLE)

WHA ...
A STRATEGY GUIDE FOR THE BOSS!?
THE NPC SHOP IN THE SQUARE JUST GOT THEM IN...

THE RAT HAS A BOSS GUIDE!?
ZAWA (MURMUR)
ZAWA
BUT WE JUST FOUND THE BOSS CHAMBER ...
HOW DID THE INFORMATION GET OUT SO QUICKLY...?
ZAWA

SHE'S REALLY GOING OUT ON A LIMB...

THE BOSS'S NAME.
SWORD SKILLS.
ESTIMATED HP.
ATTACK DAMAGE.
EVEN HIS ACCOMPANYING MOBS...

THE INFORMATION IS IMPRESSIVE.

PARA (FLIP) PARA

THIS IS VERY USEFUL.
THE BOSS'S NUMERICAL STATS AREN'T TOO DANGEROUS.
OOOH!
SEEMS THAT WAY.
WHAT!? NOW WAIT JUST A DAMN SECOND!

LOOKIT THIS HERE!
I KNEW IT!
THE INFORMANT KNOWS WHO'S A BETA TESTER!
!!!Warning!!!
This information is from the SAO beta test.
Details may not match the current version of the game.
IN FACT...
...I BET THE RAT MUST BE A BETA TESTER HERSELF.
MAYBE WE NEED TA GO HAVE A LIL CHAT, EH?

YEAH...
ARE WE REALLY GONNA TRUST INTEL FROM BETA TESTERS?
THEY COULD BE LEAVING OUT THE MOST IMPORTANT INFO TO SCREW US OVER!
ザワ
ZAWA (MURMUR)
YEAH, THEY MIGHT SAVE ALL THE BEST MORSELS FOR THEMSELVES!
ザワ
ZAWA

IF THIS CAME FROM TESTERS...
ズカ
ZUKA (STOMP)
ズカ
ZUKA
...MAYBE THEY SHOULD STAND AT THE FRONT OF THE BATTLE AND PROVE IT'S TRUE!

WHERE DID SHE GO!?
YEAH! WHERE'S THE RAT!? SHE WAS JUST HERE!
DID SHE TURN TAIL AND RUN!?
...NO!

SO TELL ME...
WHAT ARE YOU PRO-POSING WE DO ...
...OTHER THAN BE GRATEFUL FOR THE INFO?

IT'S...A GIRL!!!!!
MOJI (FIDGET)
モジモジ
MOJI
IS SHE CUTE...?
BIKU (FLINCH)
ビクッ
BIKU
ビクッ
SHE HAS A NICE FIGURE...
BUT SHE'S JUST ANOTHER GAME-ADDICT LOSER. NO USE GETTING OUR HOPES UP...
SHE'S COR-RECT!!!

IN-DEED.

IT'S GOING TO SAVE US ALL THE RECON-NAISSANCE MISSIONS.

WE MIGHT BE ABLE TO WIN WITHOUT ANY FATALI-TIES.

IN FACT...

...WE WILL DO SO.

IF THERE'S ANY FAULT IN THE INFORMATION, AS YOU SAY...

...THEN I'LL TAKE IT UPON MYSELF TO PROTECT THE GROUP.

ON MY PRIDE AS A KNIGHT ...

DON (THUD)

...I SWEAR THIS TO YOU!

SEEMS FIT-TING.
GIVEN THAT WE HAVE A PRIN-CESS.
BIBIKU (FLINCH)
HE'S LEADER-SHIP MATERIAL FOR A MAJOR GUILD DOWN THE ROAD...

ALL RIGHT, I THINK IT'S TIME TO START PLANNING!
FIRST WE HAVE TO FORM A PROPER RAID PARTY.
FI-NALLY ...
NOW TEAM UP WITH YOUR FRIENDS AND OTHERS AROUND YOU.
WHA—!?
KO (TOK)
KO
YUUKI-SAN'S IN OUR FIELD TRIP GROUP?
HEH, HEH, ISN'T THAT COOL?
I DUNNO, I BET SHE HAS NO GOOD STORIES TO TELL.
AND ALL THE GUYS WILL TRY TO PICK HER UP.
I KNOW WHAT YOU MEAN ...
I DON'T WANT TO FEEL LIKE HER WINGMAN. I'LL LOSE ALL MY SELF-CONFIDENCE...

ZULIN (DUMM)
ZUUN
ズィーン
WAI (CHATTER)
ワイワイ
WAI
OKAY, LET'S DO THIS!
YEAH!
GAYA (YAMMER)
GAYA
ガヤガヤ
AW-RIGHT! ♪
WANNA TEAM UP?
SO ...
...YOU GOT LEFT OUT TOO—
I MEAN, NO, YOU DIDN'T!
OF COURSE NOT... HA-HA ...
HEY, I KNOW!
WHY DON'T YOU TEAM UP WITH ME?
NO THANKS.
BUT... YOU KNOW ...
...WE CAN'T JOIN THE RAID UNLESS WE'RE IN A PARTY.

...I MIGHT CONSIDER IT...

BUT...

...IF YOU SEND ME THE INVITE.

OH ... RE-ALLY?

OKAY, THERE YOU GO...

ポチ

POCHI (CLICK)

YOU WERE SAYING SOMETHING BEFORE WE GOT HERE.
I COULDN'T HEAR IT THROUGH THE WIND.

IF WE BOTH SURVIVE THE BATTLE...
...TELL ME AGAIN.

KO (TOK)
KO
SO YOU TWO ARE IN YOUR OWN PARTY?
FUI (SPIN)
UH... YEAH.
FORGIVE ME!
ZUZA (SLIDE)
BA (WHOOSH)
CAN I ASK YOU TO BACK UP THE TEAM HANDLING THE BOSS'S KOBOLD GUARDS?

I GUESS WE DON'T HAVE ANY OTHER OPTION. WE DON'T HAVE THE NUMBERS FOR A FULL RAID PARTY, AFTER ALL.
WHEW.
THANKS FOR UNDER-STANDING.
AND YOU CAN'T JUST IGNORE THOSE CRONIES.
IT'S AN IMPOR-TANT JOB.

I SEE.
BUT ...

AS A KNIGHT, I'M JEALOUS...
...THAT YOU GET TO GUARD THE PRINCESS.
HA-HA. YEAH...
IT'S...AN IMPORTANT JOB...

WELL...
...THAT SHOULD DO IT.
WE TACKLE THE BOSS TWO DAYS FROM NOW.
MEET AGAIN HERE AT EIGHT IN THE MORNING.
USE TOMORROW TO REST UP.
OR PRACTICE IN YOUR TEAM IF YOU WISH.
OR JUST GET TO KNOW EACH OTHER.
IT'S ALL UP TO YOU.

ANY TEAM THAT WANTS TO JOIN TEAM A'S PRACTICE, STICK AROUND.
OTHERWISE, DISMISSED!

ZORO (TRUDGE)
ZORO
HUH?
SUTA (STOMP)
SUTA
MISS FENCER?

DON'T YOU WANT TO JOIN THE PRACTICE SESSION?
TSUKA
TSUKA (TROMP)
TSUKA

AN "IM-PORTANT JOB"? YOU'RE KIDDING.
AND WE'RE ONLY THE BACKUP HENCHMEN KILLERS?
IF WE'RE NOT A BIG PART OF THEIR PLAN, THEY SHOULD JUST SAY SO.

TSUKA
WHAT ELSE CAN WE DO? THERE'S ONLY TWO OF US.
TSUKA
WE CAN'T EVEN SWITCH IN AND LAST LONG ENOUGH FOR POT ROTATION...

PITA (PAUSE)
BIKU (FLINCH)

SWITCH ...?

POT ROTA...

WHAT?

TELL YOU WHAT.

TOMORROW, I'LL EXPLAIN PARTY COMBAT.

THERE'S A GOOD QUEST TO PRACTICE THAT.

BUT IT'S ONLY ACTIVE IN THE MORNING.

I'D LIKE TO AT LEAST GO OVER THE BASICS TONIGHT...
...SO WE COULD STOP AT A NEARBY PUB—
BISHI (SMACK)
NO.
SUTA (TROMP)
SUTA
I DON'T WANT TO BE SEEN WITH YOU.
GUSA (STAB)

WELL.
IF YOU'D PREFER A LOCATION WHERE NO ONE WILL SEE US...
...AN NPC HOUSE IS OUT, BECAUSE ANYONE CAN WALK IN...
TSUKA (STOMP)
TSUKA

!
HEY, I KNOW!

YOUR ROOM OR MINE?
WE CAN LOCK THE DOOR, AND THE WALLS ARE SOUND-PROOF.
BA (SPIN)
FURU (SHAKE)
FURU
ABSO-LUTELY NOT!
WHAT IS WRONG WITH YOU!? DISGUSTING!

KURU (SPIN)
SUTA (TEK)
SUTA

HAH!
WELL, I DIDN'T WANT TO HANG OUT IN THAT CRAPPY OLD INN EITHER.

SUTA
SUTA

MY PLACE IS PRETTY CHEAP AT EIGHTY COL A NIGHT...
...PLUS, IT'S AN ENTIRE SPACIOUS FLOOR TO MYSELF, WITH ALL-YOU-CAN-DRINK MILK!

SUTA
SUTA
SUTA

THERE'S EVEN A BATHTUB, THOUGH I BARELY EVER USE IT...

GYUA (ZWOOM)

BUWA (WHOOSH)
WHAT?
WHAT DID YOU JUST SAY??
HUH? WHAT?
THE ENTIRE FLOOR?
NOT THAT!
PLENTY OF MILK?
NOT THAT EITHER!
YOU MEAN ...
...THE BATH?

#004: Electronic Signals

WOWWW...♥

チョロー

CHORO (SPLISH)

トポ

TOPO (BLUP)

トポ

TOPO

トポ

TOPO

WELL...

ENJOY ...

下着全解除

ちゃぷ…
CHAPU (SPLISH)
...AH...

ZAPPAAAN
(SPLASH)
JABAAA
(SLOSH)
ジャバ——・・・
PUKA
(BOB)
プカ

AAAAAHHHHHH

ビクッ

BIKU (FLINCH)

—WITH THIS, I'LL HAVE NOTHING LEFT TO REGRET.

EVEN IF I DIE IN THE BOSS FIGHT...

...AND DISAPPEAR FROM THIS WORLD FOREVER...

GUUU (HRRG)

ACTU-ALLY...

...IF I HAD THE OPPORTU-NITY...

...I COULD GO FOR ONE MORE ROLL OF BREAD WITH CREAM...

BUN (SHAKE)

BUN

I KNOW HOW IT WORKS.

...AND THIS WATER ...

THAT FLA-VOR...

...ARE JUST A SERIES OF ELECTRONIC SIGNALS COMING THROUGH THE NERVEGEAR.

CHAPA (SPLISH)

IT'S ALL ABSOLUTELY FAKE.

ALL THOSE FULL-COURSE ORGANIC MEALS...
...OR THE VIRTUAL ROLL OF BREAD.
WHICH ONE SHOULD I CALL...
...THE REAL THING?

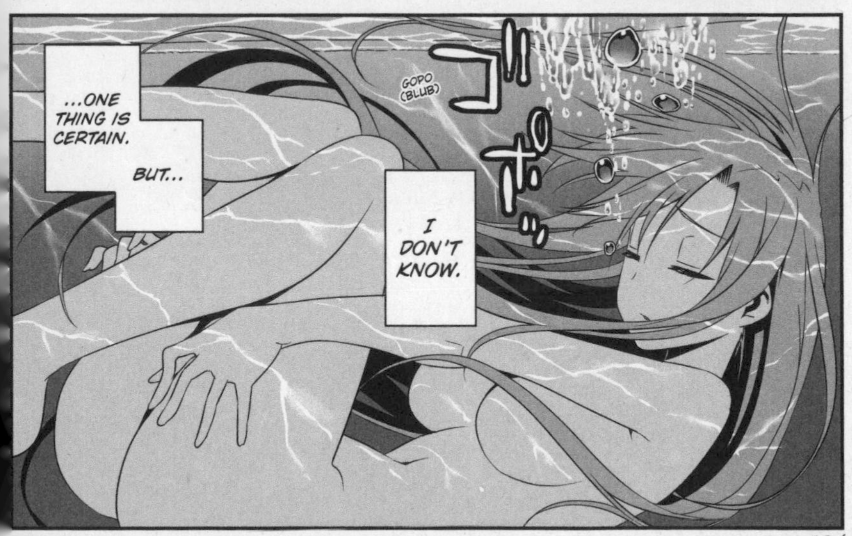
GOPO (BLUB)
I DON'T KNOW.
BUT...
...ONE THING IS CERTAIN.

THAT EVEN IN THE FACE OF DEATH...
...I CANNOT HELP BUT DESIRE...
...THESE SIMPLE ELEC-TRONIC SIGNALS.
I CAN'T SIMPLY LAUGH THAT OFF.

KON (TAP)
KO
KO
KON
BIBIKU (FLINCH)
BASA (FLOP)

KIRITTO (SERIOUS)
......
SAO Strategy Guide
F. BOSS

THAT RHYTHM ...!
GACHA (CLICK)
W-WELL, WELL...
STRANGE TO SEE YOU VISIT ME DIRECTLY.
HEY.
IS A-CHAN THE FENCER HERE?

I GOT A TIP FROM THE GIRL-STARVED GAMER NERDS BACK AT THE SQUARE...
...THAT THE TWO OF YOU WALKED OFF HAND IN HAND.
I THOUGHT YOU MIGHT HAVE ALREADY SNUCK HER IN HERE...
WH—
WHAT MAKES YOU SAY THAT?

AS IF THAT STRONG-WILLED FENCER...
NOPE, NOPE!
...WOULD EVER COME VISIT MY ROOM ON THE DAY SHE MET ME, JUST TO TAKE A BATH!

BATH?

LOOK, THAT'S HIM...
HE HITS ON EVERY GIRL IN THE GAME, TRYING TO TAKE THEM HOME WITH HIM!
WHAT A CREEP ...
I HEAR HE LURES A LOT OF THEM IN WITH SWEETS AND HIS BATH.
THE PIG...
ZOWA (SHIVER)

MMM?
UH, I MEAN ...
YES, WE LEFT TO-GETHER ...
...BUT I'D GUESS SHE'S BACK AT THE INN BY NOW MAYBE?
AHA HA HA HA!
HMM ...

WELL, NOW THAT I'M HERE...
...MIGHT AS WELL GIVE YOU THE LATEST REPORT.
PARDON ME.
AH! HEY!
EX-QUEEZE ME.
HEY, THIS ROOM IS BIG!

I COULD SELL THE DETAILS ON THIS PLACE FOR GOOD MONEY.
WHAT'S THE RENT? ANY UNIQUE EVENTS OR CONDITIONS?
HMM? WHAT'S THIS OTHER DOOR?
BATH... ROOM ...?
GIKU (FLINCH)
NOW I'M STUNNED.
THIS PLACE EVEN HAS A BATH!
Bathroom
I CAN CHARGE A LOT FOR THIS SCOOP!
ESPECIALLY TO THE GIRLS!

UM, ER...
THAT'S, UH... UNDER MAINTE-NANCE!
IT'S BROKEN! GOTTA COMPLETE A REALLY ANNOYING REPAIR QUEST BEFORE YOU CAN USE IT...

I SEE. THAT'S A SHAME...
SORRY. WANT A DRINK?

AH! HEY!
WHOA!
GASHI (SNAG)
PSYCH.
HYUGO (SWOOSH)
GUI (TUG)

ZURU (SLIP)
URG!

GACK!
ZUDAMU (THWAM)
NOW LET'S TAKE A LOOK.
GACHA (CLICK)

...NOW HERE'S A SUR-PRISE.

SOOO (PEEK)

ERM... SO...
IS *THAT*...
...PART OF YOUR STARTER EQUIPMENT?

KII-
BOY...
IT WAS NICE KNOWIN' YA.
SHUN (SHNK)
AAAAA-AAAAA-AAAAH-HHHHH-HHHHH-HHH!!
WAIT...!
NO—
BUTSUN (CLICK)

PIKI (CRAKK)

PAAN (POW)

CHAKIN (CHK)
チャキン

HAA.
HAA.
N-NICE WORK.
PACHI (CLAP)
パチパチ
PACHI

SO THAT'S THE GENERAL FLOW OF SWITCH-OUT TEAM FIGHTING.
EXCEPT FOR HOW YOU DID EVERYTHING YOURSELF WITHOUT SWITCHING.
DID YOU SAY SOME-THING?
ME? NO.

ANYWAY, YOU SHOULD CHECK YOUR LOOTED ITEMS.

—A SWORD ...?

YEP.

THAT'S A "WIND FLEURET."

SHUN (SHHK)

IT'S A GREAT SWORD FOR A FENCER, BEING SO WEIGHTED TOWARD AGILITY AND PRECISION.
IT'S MUCH, MUCH BETTER THAN THE IRON RAPIERS YOU BUY FROM THE SHOPS...

IT'S BEAUTIFUL...
AHEM.
GYOKUN (GA-BING)
NOW YOU JUST NEED TO UPGRADE IT IN TOWN.

AFTER ALL THAT TIME IN THE LABYRINTH, YOU MUST HAVE ENOUGH MATERIALS TO GET IT TO PLUS FOUR.
I CAN SHOW YOU TO A GOOD BLACK-SMITH.
AH.
THANK YOU...
UM, HOW MUCH WILL I OWE YOU—
NO CHARGE.

I'M THE ONE WHO OWES YOU.

I'M SURE YOU'D HAVE PREFERRED TO STAY OUT OF SIGHT BACK THERE.

THANKS.

SO.
IF WE'RE GOING BACK TO TOWN...

...YOU COULD MAYBE USE THE COL FROM THE OTHER LOOT TO FILL OUT YOUR EQUIPMENT.
WHAT DO YOU SAY, SENSEI?
HEAR THAT?
LUCKY YOU, A-CHAN! YOU'LL HAVE EXTRA MONEY!
HMM.
A SPEED-FIRST FENCER DOESN'T WANT BIG ARMOR SLOWING HER DOWN.
AHH, GOOD POINT.
......

KAAN (CLANG)

MUCH OBLIGED!
......
COOL, IT WORKED.
SO IT SEEMS.

NOW IT'S A WIND FLEURET PLUS FOUR.
HOW DOES IT FEEL?
HMF!
IT'S MUCH LIGHTER NOW.
HMF!
HYUN (SWISH)
IT DOESN'T WOBBLE ANY-MORE.
HYUN
HYUN
BE CARE-FUL.
BE CARE-FUL.
BE

WOW, SHE'S GOT A GOOD EYE FOR WEAPONRY.
YEAH, WE SHOULD COMPLI-MENT HER MORE.

CAN THIS...
...GO UP TO PLUS FIVE?
YEAH.

THE MATERIALS TO GET IT TO PLUS FIVE ARE ON THE SECOND—

YOU CAN'T GET WHAT YOU NEED FOR IT ON THE FIRST FLOOR.

...YEAH.

WHAT SHE SAID.

OH... TOO BAD.

TOMORROW AT TEN.

I HAVE SOMETHING ELSE TO BUY, SO I'LL SEE YOU LATER.
チャキン
CHAKIN (CHK)

COME BACK SOON.
ギィ
GII (CREAK)
バタン
BATAN (THUMP)

...!

Lingerie Shop

FOUND IT...!

GU
(PUMP)

AAAH!

DON'T WORRY.
I'LL PUT YOUR PURCHASE IN MY HIGHEST-PRICED TIER OF INFORMATION.
I'LL EVEN PAY YOU ROYALTIES ON EACH SALE.
ALSO, WHICH PANTIES ARE FOR THE BIG DAY?
BIG DAY—
WHY WOULD I—!? WHO NEEDS THOSE IN A GAME!?

OH? YOU DON'T KNOW, A-CHAN?
THE GAME'S MORAL CODE CAN BE REMOV...

...!

?

I MEANT ...
...THE "BIG DAY" AGAINST THE BOSS, OF COURSE.
WHY?
WHAT DID YOU THINK I WAS REFERRING TO, A-CHAN?
BA (SPIN)
O-OH, LOOK, THAT ONE'S KIND OF CUTE!!
YES! RED AND WHITE, THAT'S PERFECT!
EXCUSE ME, CAN I TRY THESE ON?

ALL I SAID... WAS THAT I WANTED TO KNOW WHERE OUR BEAUTIFUL COMPANION WAS GOING SHOPPING.

HERE, A THOUSAND COL.
ポン
PON (BING)
チャリンッ
CHARIN (CLINK)
THANK YOU.

HUH?
YOU DIDN'T WANT TO KNOW WHAT SHE BOUGHT?

HEH.
YOU MIGHT REGRET IT.

SUNDAY, DECEMBER 4TH, FOUR WEEKS AFTER THE GAME OF DEATH BEGAN.

THE DAY...

カチャ
KACHA (CLANK)
カチャ
KACHA
...OF OUR FIRST BOSS BATTLE.

GOOD MORNING, MISS FENCER!
LET'S DO OUR BEST TODAY!
ツッカーーン
TSUKKAN (KA-DING)
!
NICE.
GOOD CHOICE!
AH, I SEE.
YESTERDAY, SHE HAD...
IT'S ONLY...
BA (WHOOSH)
...FOR THE BOSS BATTLE! NOTHING MORE!
...OKAY??

#005: Talwar

THAT'S ALL FROM ME.
ANY LAST QUES-TIONS?
ヒョイ
HYOI (SWISH)
GO AHEAD.
JUST ONE.
WHAT HAPPENS IF THE INTEL FROM THE BETA TEST STRATEGY GUIDE IS DIFFERENT FROM WHAT HAPPENS?

DIAVEL.
CAN I ASSUME THAT AS THE LEADER...
...YOU WILL GIVE THE ORDER TO RETREAT?

OF COURSE. HUMAN LIFE IS THE TOP PRIORITY.
BUT OUR SIMULATED BATTLE STRATEGY WAS PERFECT.
WE'RE NOT GOING TO LET ANYONE DIE.

DON'T EVEN PAY 'EM NO MIND, SIR DIAVEL.
KEH!
THEY JUST DUNNO WHAT KINDA LEADER YOU ARE.
ONLY REASON THEY'D BE SO SKEPTI-CAL.

MAYBE IF THEY'D TAKEN PART IN THE TRAINING SESSION RATHER 'N FLIRTIN' UP A STORM, THEY'D KNOW.
WATCH IT, KIBA-CCHI!
HA-HA-HA!
...

THANK YOU FOR YOUR HIGH PRAISE. BUT I'D BE NERVOUS IF WE DIDN'T HAVE THIS EXACT RAID PARTY.
YOU'RE THE BEST DAMN GROUP I COULD POSSIBLY HOPE FOR.

LET'S WIN THIS THING.

C'MON.
LET'S GO!
GI (CREAAAAK)
LISTEN UP.
DON'T GET COCKY. KNOW YER PLACE.
GI
GI
GI
GOHHH (WHOOSH)
GI
GI

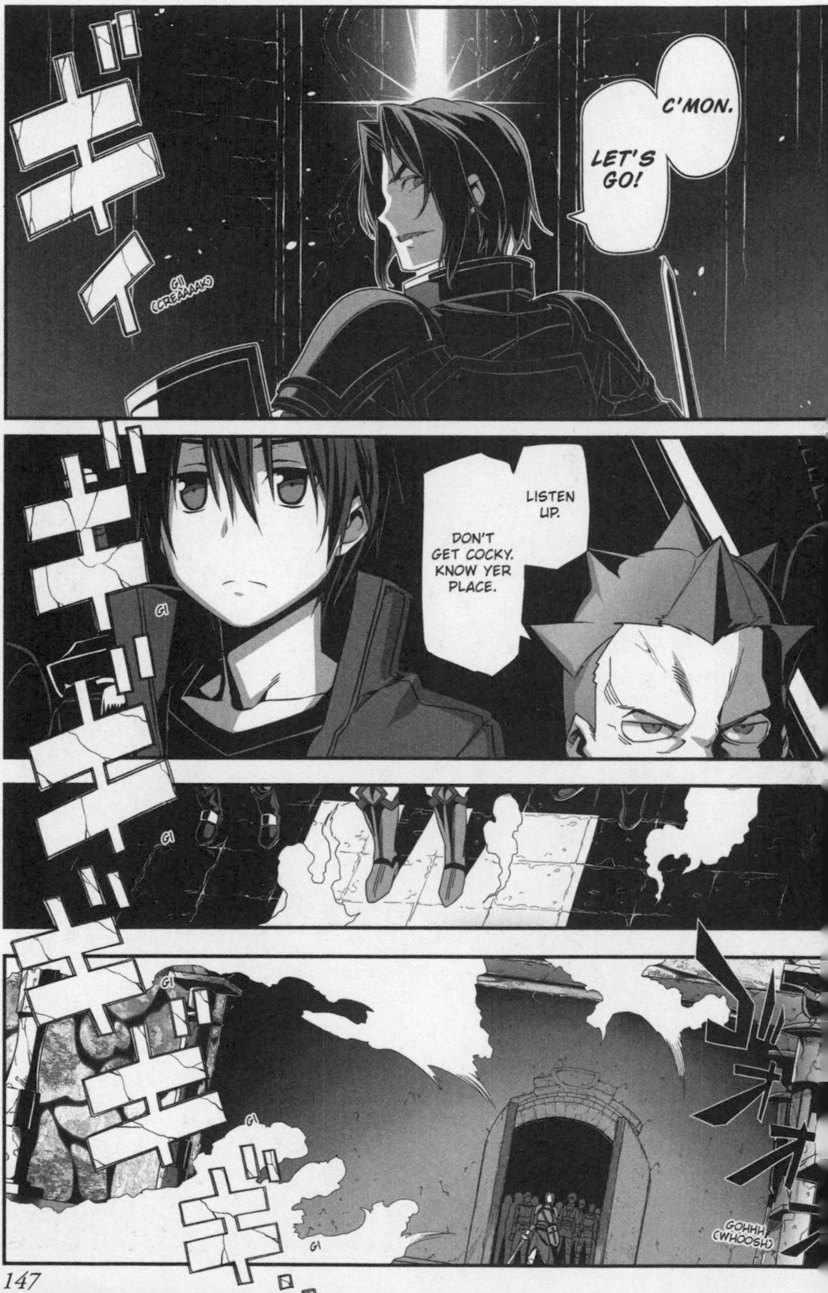

GO
GO
GRRMMM
GO
GO
GO
THERE HE IS...
GO
GO
GO

THE KING OF KOBOLDS, BOSS OF THE FIRST FLOOR...
ZUZUUN (ZDUMM)
...ILL-FANG, THE KOBOLD LORD!!

HIS MAIN WEAPON IS A BONE AX. BACKUP IS A TALWAR! ACCOMPANIED BY THREE SENTINELS!
IT ALL MATCH-ES THE INTEL! AND WE CAN WIN THIS THING!!
FOLLOW MY LEAD!!!
YEAH!!!

DO (STOMP)
DO
DO
DO
...
THE HENCH-MEN ARE ON THE MOVE! WHAT ARE YOU WAITING FOR!?

Y-YEAH...
CHAKI (CHK)

WAA (RAHH)

ALL RIGHT!

THE BOSS IS IN PATTERN C!

OOOOO
(ROAAAH)
COMMENCE ATTACK!!

TANK TEAM A, PULL BACK!

TEAM D, ADVANCE!!

TEAM B, PREPARE FOR THE NEXT PATTERN!

AYE-AYE!

INCREDIBLE. EVEN AGAINST THIS GIGANTIC MONSTER...

...WITH THE THREAT OF DEATH HANGING OVER OUR HEADS...

SWITCH!!
WAAAA (RAHHH)
KIIN (CLANG)
DON (BOOM)
DOKA (WHAM)
THEY'RE ALL...
...SO TOUGH!
MMMG!!!
I TOLDJA, DRINK THAT DAMN POT!
HUR-RY!
JIRI (PAUSE)
JIRI
GLUG, GLUG!
HURRY!
BUT TOUGHER THAN ANYONE ELSE—
S-SWI...

SWITCH.

BURU (SHIVER)
ぶるっ

BIKU (TWITCH)
BIKU
BIKU
KARA (CLICK)
カラカラ
KARA
KYUPO (SHUNK)
PAAAN (POW)

I TOLDJA, DON'T GET COCKY.

I'VE HEARD ALL ABOUT HOW YA STOLE ALL THE LAST-ATTACK BONUSES ON THE BOSSES IN THE BETA.
THE TALE OF THE SWORDS-MAN WITHOUT A SHIELD.

I FIGURE YOU'RE AFTER THAT LAST ATTACK ON THIS ONE TOO.
BUT THAT AIN'T —
MISS FENCER?
WATCH OUT, THE SECOND WAVE OF SENTINELS ARE A HIGHER LEVEL.
WE'RE UP.
O-OKAY!

TOTETE (TEK)

OOOH!

BA

バッ

BA (SPIN)

HERE COMES HIS SECONDARY WEAPON, THE TALWAR!
EVERYONE REMEMBER WHAT TO DO?
GURUOOO (GRAAHH)
THE BASIC'S THE SAME: DEFLECT THE WEAPON, HIT HIS THROAT!!

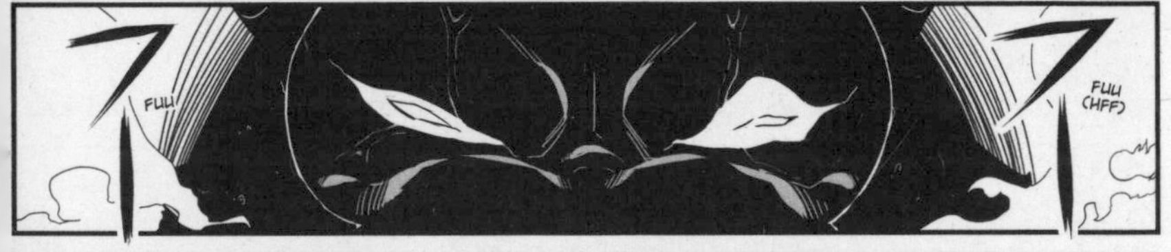

SHARAN (SHING)

UM, DO YOU KNOW WHAT A TALWAR LOOKS LIKE?

HUH? ISN'T THAT A KIND OF SWORD...

...FROM SOUTH ASIA...?

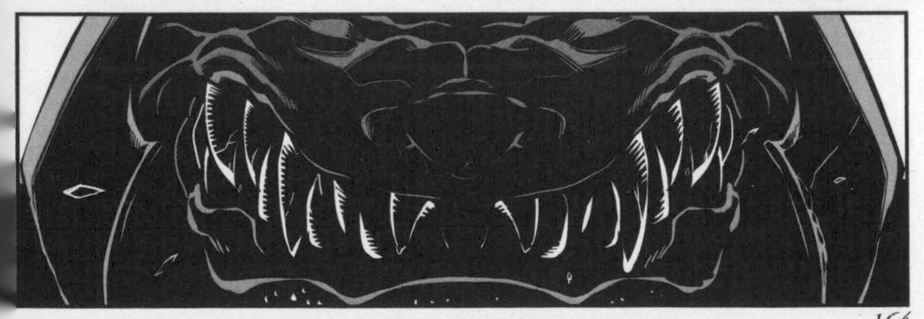

NO! GET BACK!!
JAKI (SHKING)
HEY, NOT SO FAST!
YOU THAT DESPERATE FOR THE L.A. BONUS?
IT BELONGS TA SIR DIAVEL, PUNK!
NO INTERFERIN', NOW!
DON'T BE CRAZY!!
YOU HAVE TO STOP THEM!
HIS BACKUP WEAPON...
...IS A KATANA!!
THAT KOBOLD LORD...
...IS DIFFERENT FROM THE BETA!!!
GUWA (WHOOSH)
SO IT'S TRUE!
FROM THE BETA ...?

DIAVE-
EEEL!!

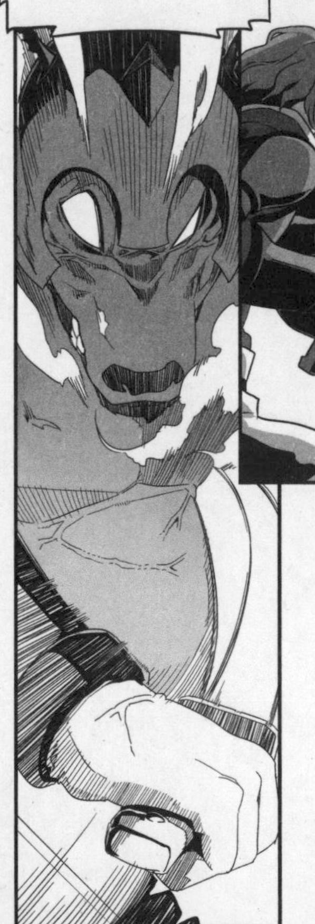
GET
AWAAAAY
!!!!!

A STUN EFFECT !!

ZUSHIN (WHUD)

GACHI (RATTLE) ガチ GACHI ガチ

ZUSHIN

GAGI
(KCHANG)
S...
SIR DIAVEL!!!

DADA (DASH)

HURRY UP, TANKS! HE'S GONNA ATTACK AGAIN!

TAKE CARE OF TEAM C, THEY'RE KNOCKED OUT!

WE'RE ON IT!

BUT WHAT ABOUT YOU?

YOUR EQUIP-MENT'S TOO LIGHT TO...

ZUPAN (KAPOW)
WHA ...!
THEY'RE SO FAST!

GOOD!!

DEFLECT HIS WEAPON!

I'LL STRIKE HIS THROAT!!

THIS SHOULD DO IT!!!

ZAN (ZSHH)

NO, DIA-VEL!
PITA (PAUSE)
FOCUS ON DE-FENSE!!

DIA-VEL!

KYUIIII
(WHRRRR)
DON'T START...
...YOUR SKILL MOTION !!

[To be continued in Volume 2]

Nice to meet you. I'm Kiseki Himura.
Thank you so much for checking out this book.
As a sign of my gratitude, please accept
this beautiful girl in a bathing suit.
Do enjoy.

...Enlarged?
Whatever do you mean?

<Acknowledgments>
This series was only possible through
the help of the following people.

Original Work:
Reki Kawahara-sensei
abec-sensei

Art:
Murasan-san
Nazu Natsuki-san
Kasutera-san

Editor:
Kentarou Ogino-san

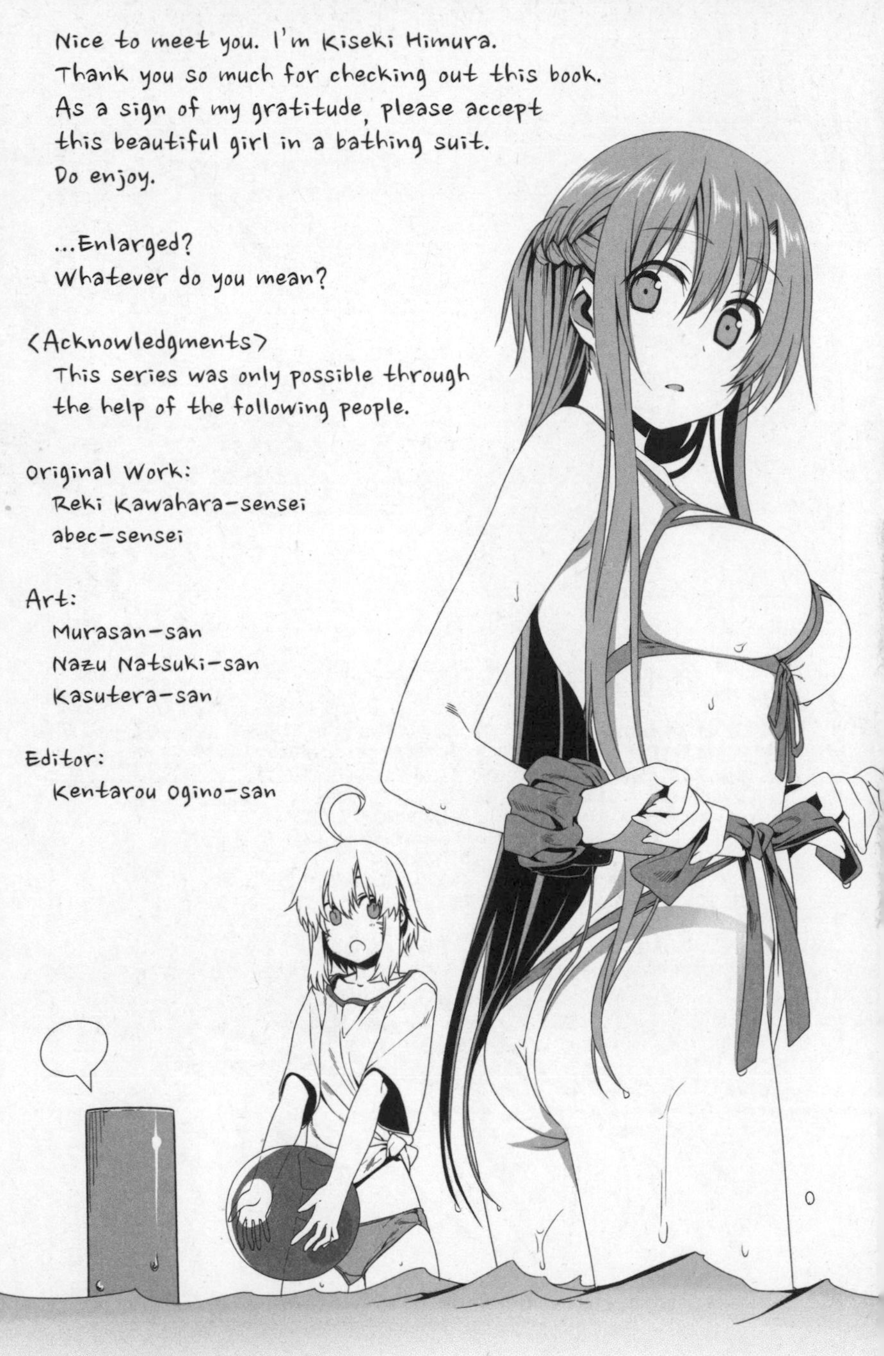

MESSAGE

ORIGINAL STORY

REKI KAWAHARA

CONGRATULATIONS ON THE RELEASE OF THE FIRST GRAPHIC NOVEL!
AS THE CREATOR OF THIS STORY, I COULDN'T BE MORE PLEASED BY THE POWER OF THE MANGA MEDIUM TO PORTRAY STUNNING ACTION SCENES, SUBTLE CHARACTER DEPICTIONS, AND THE FINE PACING OF DIALOGUE. I BET IF THIS SERIES HAD BEEN FOR SALE IN AINCRAD, ASUNA WOULD BE SAYING, "I CAN'T DIE UNTIL I READ NEXT MONTH'S CHAPTER!"
ONE LAST THING! PLEASE, ANIPLEX: HELP HIMURA-SAN'S VERSION OF *SAO: PROGRESSIVE* BECOME ITS OWN ANIME SERIES!

reki

MESSAGE abec

CHARACTER DESIGN

abec

CONGRATS ON THE FIRST VOLUME! HIMURA-SAN'S INCREDIBLE ART HAS BROUGHT THE STORY OF THE EARLY DAYS OF AINCRAD TO LIFE IN WAYS BOTH COOL AND CUTE! I CAN'T WAIT TO READ MORE. ASUNA IS SO CUTE IN A MORE *TSUNDERE* FORM! SINCERE CONGRATULATIONS FROM ABEC, ILLUSTRATOR OF THE ORIGINAL NOVEL SERIES.

TSUNDERE: *A TERM COMBINING THE WORDS* TSUN-TSUN *AND* DERE-DERE *AND REFERRING TO A CHARACTER WHO'S PRICKLY ON THE OUTSIDE ("TSUN") BUT SHY AND SENTIMENTAL UNDERNEATH ("DERE.")*

SWORD ART ONLINE: PROGRESSIVE 1

ART: KISEKI HIMURA
ORIGINAL STORY: REKI KAWAHARA
CHARACTER DESIGN: ABEC

Translation: Stephen Paul
Lettering: Brndn Blakeslee & Lys Blakeslee

Edited by ASCII MEDIA WORKS
First published in Japan in 2014 by KADOKAWA CORPORATION, Tokyo.
English translation rights arranged with KADOKAWA CORPORATION, Tokyo, through Tuttle-Mori Agency, Inc., Tokyo.

Yen Press
Hachette Book Group
1290 Avenue of the Americas
New York, NY 10104

www.HachetteBookGroup.com
www.YenPress.com

Yen Press is an imprint of Hachette Book Group, Inc. The Yen Press name and logo are trademarks of Hachette Book Group, Inc.

First Yen Press Edition: January 2015

ISBN: 978-0-316-25937-8

10 9 8 7 6

BVG

Printed in the United States of America